Pacific Crest Middle School
3030 NW Elwood Lane
Bend, OR 97703

THE OUTER PLANETS

by Giles Sparrow

Smart Apple Media

Published by Smart Apple Media
P.O. Box 3263, Mankato, Minnesota 56002

Printed in the United States of America at Corporate
Graphics, in North Mankato, Minnesota.

Published by arrangement with the
Watts Publishing Group Ltd., London.

Library of Congress Cataloging-in-Publication Data
Sparrow, Giles.
 The outer planets / by Giles Sparrow.
   p. cm. -- (Space travel guides)
 Includes bibliographical references and index.
 Summary: "Presents an imaginary tour of the outer
 solar system's "gas giants" Jupiter, Saturn, Uranus,
 and Neptune and explores some of their major
 moons. Provides statistics, diagrams, and information about the planets' physical properties and
 conditions"--Provided by publisher.
 ISBN 978-1-59920-664-6 (library binding)
 1. Outer planets--Juvenile literature. I. Title.
 QB659.S73 2012
 523.4--dc22

                        2010032768

1511
7-2012

9 8 7 6 5 4 3 2

Conceived and produced by Tall Tree Ltd
Cartoons: Guy Harvey

Picture credits:
t-top, b-bottom, l-left, r-right, c-center
All images courtesy of NASA, except:
26cr istockphoto.com/tpuerzer

Disclaimer
The web site addresses (URLs) included in this book
were valid at the time of going to press. However,
because of the nature of the Internet, it is possible
that some addresses have changed, or sites may
have changed or closed down since publication.
While the author and publisher regret any
inconvenience this may cause to readers, no
responsibility for any such changes can be
accepted by either the author or the publisher.

This book describes a fictional journey into outer
space. It is not possible for humans to travel to
the inner planets with present-day technology.
Readers are invited to use their imaginations to
journey around our solar system.

Words in **bold** are in the glossary on page 30

Contents

NEPTUNE
30.1 AU FROM SUN

URANUS
19.2 AU FROM SUN

SATURN
9.5 AU FROM SUN

JUPITER
5.2 AU FROM SUN

The Outer Solar System

Get ready to blast off on the trip of a lifetime! We're going exploring into cold, dark, and dangerous territory to the outer reaches of the **solar system**. The solar system consists of our nearest star (the Sun) and everything that circles around it.

SOLAR SYSTEM CENTER

The Sun is an enormous ball of exploding gas much larger than any **planet**. Like all heavy objects, it produces a pull called **gravity**. This pull stops fast-moving objects from flying off into space and instead traps them in circular or oval paths called **orbits**.

INNER AND OUTER SOLAR SYSTEM

The inner solar system is home to relatively small, rocky planets—Mercury, Venus, Earth, and Mars—and is surrounded by the asteroid belt, a ring of small, rocky objects. The inner solar system is tiny compared to the vast expanse of the outer solar system, and the rocky planets are also tiny compared to their outer neighbors. We'll be visiting the giant outer **worlds**—Jupiter, Saturn, Uranus, and Neptune—each of which is dominated by gas and ice rather than rock.

MOONS AND OTHER BODIES

Each giant planet has its own large family of **moons** in orbit around it, and we'll also be visiting many of these as we go. We will then finish our trip with a visit to the **comets** and dwarf planets—small, icy **astronomical bodies** that hang at the very edge of our solar system. Along the way, we'll learn about the unique histories, features, and hazards of these fascinating objects. It's going to be a fun trip, but be careful—it could also be a dangerous one!

MARS
1.5 AU FROM SUN

EARTH'S MOON
238,855 MILES (384,400 KM)
FROM EARTH

EARTH
1 AU FROM SUN

VENUS
0.7 AU FROM SUN

MERCURY
0.4 AU FROM SUN

ASTEROID BELT
2.8 AU FROM SUN

NEED TO KNOW

It's a long trip to the outer solar system. The Earth is 93 million miles (150 million km) from the Sun—this is one astronomical unit, or AU—but the outer planets are much farther away. The distances from the Sun are as follows: Jupiter = 5.2 AU; Saturn = 9.5 AU; Uranus = 19.2 AU; Neptune = 30.1 AU. The dwarf planet Pluto (see page 28) is 39.5 AU, and the farthest point of the collection of icy objects known as the Kuiper belt (see page 29) is about 47 AU.

Diameter: 88,846 miles (142,984 km); Mass: 318 x Earth; Day: 9.9 hours; Year: 11.88 Earth years

Jupiter

Named after the Roman king of the gods, Jupiter is the largest planet in the solar system. Earth—which has a mass of 5.97 trillion trillion kilograms—could fit inside this vast, multi-colored ball of gas 1,300 times over. Some of Jupiter's individual storms are so large they could swallow up our entire planet!

TURBULENT WORLD

Jupiter pumps out a huge amount of heat, and this drives powerful weather systems. These are stretched out into bands that wrap around the planet, giving Jupiter a striped appearance. Bands of pale, high-altitude clouds have gaps between them, revealing dark belts lower in the **atmosphere**. Huge storms create swirling reddish clouds. The most famous of these storms, the Great Red Spot, has raged for more than 300 years.

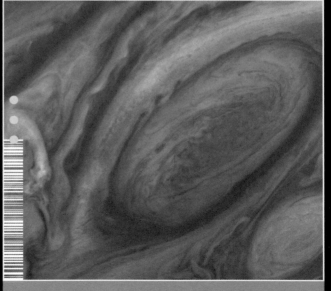

Jupiter's Great Red Spot is large enough to contain three planets the size of Earth. This huge, high-pressure storm rotates counterclockwise every six or seven days and its shape, color, and size change constantly.

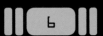

GIANT OF THE SOLAR SYSTEM

Jupiter is a "gas giant"—a world very different from solid, rocky planets like Earth. It is made up of light gases that have collected around a roughly Earth-sized rocky core. These gases make up an atmosphere hundreds of miles deep. Despite the name "gas giant," most of Jupiter's interior is actually liquid—inside the planet, the weight of gas pressing down from above squeezes the gas into a liquid. Around the core is a swirling sea of liquid hydrogen that conducts electricity and generates Jupiter's huge magnetic field —not the place for a relaxing swim!

NOT TO MISS

HAPPY FAMILY: *Jupiter has a huge family of 63 moons. Many have stretched or tilted orbits, indicating that they are asteroids that have been captured by Jupiter's strong gravity.*

MAJOR MOONS: *The four major moons (Io, Europa, Ganymede, and Callisto) are collectively known as the Galilean moons, after the Italian astronomer Galileo who discovered them in 1609–1610.*

TROJAN ASTEROIDS: *Jupiter shares its orbit with two large clouds of asteroids called Trojans.*

RINGS: *Jupiter has its own set of planetary rings (see below), but they are much paler than those around Saturn (see pages 16–17).*

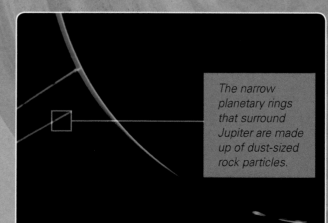

The narrow planetary rings that surround Jupiter are made up of dust-sized rock particles.

Io

Io is the innermost of Jupiter's four major moons. Io's surface looks like a burnt pizza—but you wouldn't want a bite of it! It's the most volcanic world in the solar system. Huge lava lakes constantly reshape its surface and clouds of sulfur rise high above the surface.

VOLCANO WORLD

Although Io is quite large for a moon (2,264 miles, or 3,643 km, wide), it is a fairly small astronomical body. Scientists would usually expect its rocks to have frozen solid billions of years ago. However, Io's interior has stayed molten because it orbits close to Jupiter. The giant planet's gravity tugs Io this way and that, pulling the moon's rocks so they grind against each other. This grinding produces enormous heat, melting Io's crust and creating countless **volcanoes**.

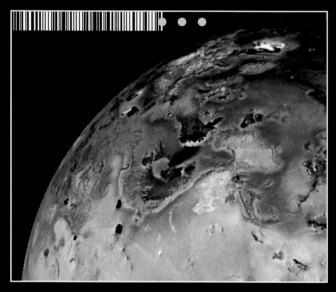

The dark spots shown here scattered around the surface of Io are active volcanoes.

TRAVELER'S TIPS - GETTING HEAVY

Even if you can avoid its volcanoes, Io is still one of the solar system's most dangerous moons. There's no real atmosphere apart from a thin haze of particles from the sulfur plumes. Io orbits in the middle of Jupiter's deadly radiation belts, where particles blowing out from the Sun are swept up in the planet's magnetic field and accelerated to high speeds. These deadly particles will pass straight through a normal space suit and cause huge damage to the cells of your body. Explorers on Io need special radiation suits made from layers of dense material, such as lead plates. Fortunately, Io's gravity is only one-fifth of that on Earth, so even if the suit is bulky, it still won't weigh much.

Io's low gravity enables the sulfur gas from this huge volcanic eruption to rise to a great height above the moon before falling back to the surface.

Io's volcanic features include lakes of molten rock, long lava flows, and **geysers** that throw out plumes of sulfur. These geysers eject clouds of gas and liquid at speeds of up to 1.9 miles (3 km) per second. The clouds can reach up to 311 miles (500 km) into the sky. Most of Io's crust is rich in sulfur. This melts more easily than the rocks on Earth and covers the landscape with reds, browns, yellows, whites, and greens. Make sure to take an up-to-date map with you because Io's surface changes rapidly and can be unrecognizable after just a few years.

NEED TO KNOW

Each one of the four "gas giant" planets has many moons. These can range in size from tiny objects a couple miles (about three kilometers) across to bodies about the size of Earth's Moon (2,160 miles, or 3,476 km, wide) or even bigger. The largest moon in the solar system is Jupiter's **satellite** Ganymede, which is 3,270 miles (5,262 km) wide. Jupiter has 63 moons, Saturn has 61, Uranus has 27, and Neptune has 13. Most of these distant worlds are made up of ice and rock.

Europa

Jupiter's second major moon is the smallest of the "big four" and just a little smaller than Earth's Moon. From space, it looks very different from Io—it appears to be as smooth as a marble. Europa's icy crust may also hide an ocean that's teeming with life.

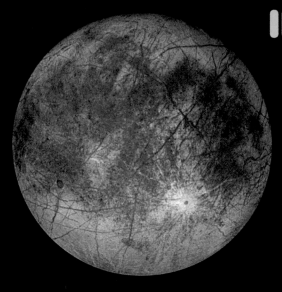

Europa's bright, pinkish-white surface is crisscrossed with countless scars.

SELF-HEALING SURFACE

Europa's surface is smooth because its icy crust is just a thin shell on top of a deep ocean of liquid water. Under the ocean, Europa is made of rock like Io, and it takes only slightly less of a pummeling from Jupiter's gravity. Undersea volcanoes keep the seas relatively warm, and whenever the surface cracks apart, warmer ice from beneath wells up to fill the gap. This freezes solid as soon it is exposed to the cold of space.

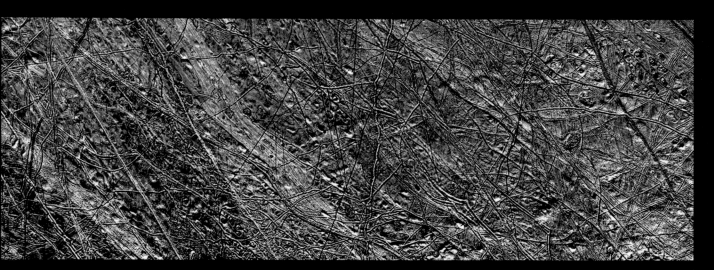

Europa's water-ice surface is covered with shallow ridges. Scientists believe they are formed when Jupiter's gravity causes the crust to crack. Escaping water freezes, creating the ridges.

According to the latest measurements, Europa's crust is several miles thick, but the ocean beneath could be up to 60 miles (100 km) deep. With deep-sea volcanoes pumping chemical nutrients into the water, Europa's seas could be an ideal place for living creatures to survive—just as they do around the deep-sea vents of Earth's own oceans. So far, it's impossible to send a probe through the ice and go alien-hunting, but perhaps that will be possible in the future!

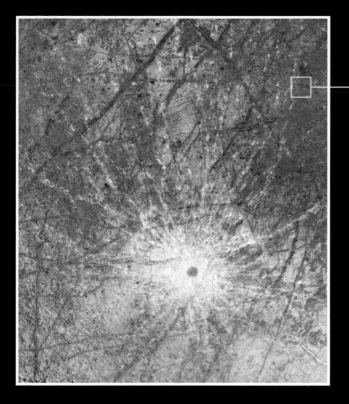

Europa's shifting crust and ocean keep the moon's surface smooth. The surface around this recent impact crater (left) is rough, but the older crater (below) has flattened out over time.

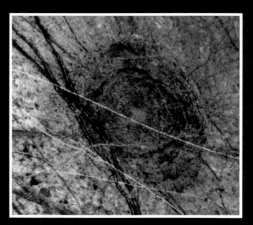

TRAVELER'S TIPS - LOOKING FOR LIFE

At the moment, it's impossible to know for sure if there is life in Europa's ocean. Any life forms there could be similar to those found in Earth's oceans—there could be Europan fish, shrimp, and even squid! The possibility of life on this icy moon makes it the solar system's most important conservation zone—if we do go looking for life, we don't want to harm it by introducing Earth-based germs or diseases. So for the foreseeable future, Europa's off limits for everything except for sterilized robots. In 2003, NASA even deliberately piloted their Galileo space probe into Jupiter's clouds to avoid the risk of polluting Europa.

Ganymede and Callisto

The outer two large moons of Jupiter are much bigger than Io and Europa, and each has its own story to tell. Ganymede was once an active world that looks like an icy equivalent of our own Earth. Callisto is probably the most heavily cratered body in the solar system.

ICY CONTINENTS

Ganymede is the largest moon in the solar system and far enough from Jupiter to be a deep-frozen ball of rock and ice. Its surface has a mix of dark and light ice patches separated by cracks and stretches. Some parts are more heavily cratered than others as they've been exposed to bombardment from space for longer. Surface cracks suggest Ganymede once orbited closer to Jupiter—the pull of the planet's gravity kept Ganymede's interior molten and allowed its icy surface to crack into **plates** like those on Earth.

Ganymede has mountains, valleys, craters, and frozen flows of icy lava. Scientists believe it may have a thin oxygen atmosphere.

Ganymede's cratered surface is icy, but its interior is rocky. It is thought that there may be a layer of liquid water between them.

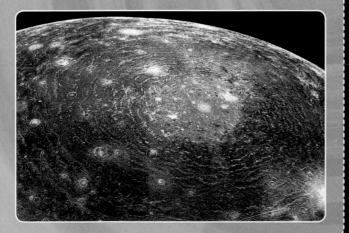

COSMIC PUNCHBAG

Callisto is a little smaller than Ganymede and quite a bit farther out from Jupiter, so the rocky, icy moon has never melted or become active. Its frozen surface has been a target for asteroids and comets over billions of years. The result is a dark moon covered in bright patches where recent craters have thrown out fresh ice from below the surface.

Diameter: 74,898 miles (120,536 km); Mass: 95 × Earth; Day: 10.66 hours; Year: 29.46 Earth years

Saturn

The gas giant Saturn is famous for its big, bright rings. This huge ball of gas and liquid is the second largest planet after Jupiter but is much lighter. In fact, it's less dense than water, so if you dropped it into a big enough bathtub, it would float!

CHANGING FACE

Saturn changes its appearance depending on the angle at which you see it. The rings extend up to 50,000 miles (80,000 km) from the equator but are only about 50 feet (15 m) thick. They disappear from view completely every 15 years when they lie "edge-on" to us. Like Jupiter, Saturn has a huge equatorial bulge—it's 10 percent wider across the middle than it is from pole to pole. Both huge planets spin so quickly that the gases they are made up of are flung outward, creating a bulge around the equator.

All the gas giants have ring systems, but Saturn's are by far the most impressive. They are made up of billions of pieces of icy material.

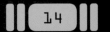

THE GREAT WHITE SPOT: *A storm that appears once every Saturn year (or every 30 Earth years)*
SIX-SIDED CLOUD: *A hexagonal-shaped cloud system around Saturn's north pole; Each side of the hexagon is 8,575 miles (13,800 km) long.*
DRAGON STORM: *A large and powerful storm that stretches around Saturn's southern hemisphere*
SATURN'S AURORAE: *Just like Earth, Saturn's powerful magnetic field deflects solar particles. These react with the atmosphere to create glowing aurorae (see below) similar to Earth's northern lights.*

When Saturn's rings lie "edge on" to Earth, they disappear from view. The first astronomers to observe this disappearance thought that Saturn was eating its own rings!

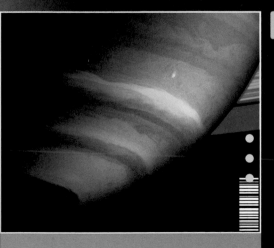

The glowing feature in the top right is a huge, raging electrical storm. The light-colored bands are layers of high atmospheric cloud, while the red bands are the lower layers.

MISTY ATMOSPHERE

With its hazy, creamy-white atmosphere, the planet Saturn looks a lot calmer than its more colorful, stormy neighbor Jupiter. But don't let this fool you—in reality, Saturn's weather is almost as turbulent as Jupiter's, but the active clouds are hidden from sight by a hazy layer of mist. Despite this, Saturn still has clear light and dark weather bands. Occasional white spots erupt to the surface, marking the tops of enormous storms raging violently beneath.

Ringed Wonder

Saturn's rings stretch out to three times the planet's width. Each circle is made up of thousands of smaller ringlets. Some scientists believe the rings are the remains of a destroyed moon, while others think they may be matter left over from the formation of Saturn.

RING STRUCTURE

Saturn's main rings are named after letters of the alphabet. From the outside in, they are the A ring, the B ring (the broadest and brightest), and the fainter C and D rings closer to the planet. The A and B rings are separated by a gap called the Cassini Divison (though this has a few ringlets within it), and the A ring is also split in two by the narrow Encke Division. Outside the A ring runs the narrow, twisted F ring, and farther out are the fuzzy G and E rings.

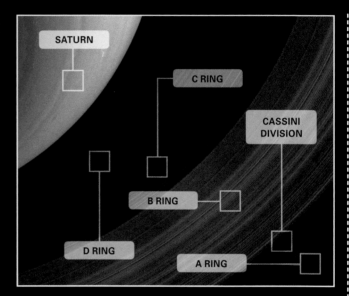

SATURN

C RING

CASSINI DIVISION

B RING

D RING

A RING

Saturn's rings extend out around the planet's equator. The densest, brightest rings are the A and B rings.

TRAVELER'S TIPS - SHEPHERDING THE RINGS

If you fly through Saturn's rings, go for the gaps where the deadly chunks of ice are fewer and farther between. In general, the pattern of gaps and rings is controlled by Saturn's many moons. Most orbit outside the rings, but their gravity still makes their influence felt. A few small "shepherd moons" orbit on either side of narrow rings, keeping their particles in place. For example, Epimetheus and Janus have a tiny ring sandwiched between their orbits. Countless tiny "moonlets" keep the ringlets that make up the main rings in place. The main structure of the rings stays the same, but there are constantly shifting patterns of spokes and twists within them.

INSIDE THE RINGS

Up close, the thousands of ringlets turn out to be streams of ice chunks, each in its own orbit around Saturn. These ring particles are kept in their circular, flattened orbits by jostling against each other and are constantly being ground down through collisions. The particles vary in size from tiny grains of dust to house-sized boulders. The rings with the largest particles, such as the B ring, are the brightest.

The ring particles collide constantly, merging to create small "moonlets" and then breaking apart. There is enough mass in the rings to make a moon that is 186 miles (300 km) wide.

Saturn's Moons

Saturn has at least 61 moons, and while most are tiny captured asteroids or comets, several are interesting bodies. They range from huge Titan (see pages 20–21), the second largest moon in the solar system, down through frozen Dione and Mimas, to tiny Enceladus.

VARIED ICEBALLS

Saturn's moons are made mostly of ice and rock. Mimas, Dione, Rhea, and Tethys are frozen balls of ice covered with many craters. Mimas has a huge crater that is the biggest in comparison to the moon's size of any crater in the whole solar system. Dione is covered in steep ice cliffs that look like bright streaks when seen from space. Hyperion is the shattered remnant of a much larger moon, and Iapetus has a strange surface that is half dark and half bright.

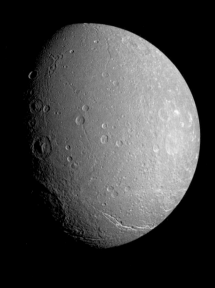

Two of Saturn's crater-scarred, icy moons—Dione (above right) and Rhea (below).

MOON DIAMETERS

JUPITER: Io = 2,264 mi (3,643 km); Europa = 1,950 mi (3,138 km); Ganymede = 3,270 mi (5,262 km); Callisto = 2,986 mi (4,806 km)

SATURN: Mimas = 260 mi (418 km); Dione = 696 mi (1,120 km); Rhea = 951 mi (1,530 km); Tethys = 657 mi (1,058 km); Hyperion = 230 mi (370 km); Enceladus = 318 mi (512 km); Iapetus = 895 mi (1,440 km); Phoebe = 137 mi (220 km); Titan = 3,200 mi (5,150 km)

URANUS: Miranda = 292 mi (470 km); Ariel = 720 mi (1,158 km); Umbriel = 727 mi (1,170 km); Titania = 981 mi (1,578 km); Oberon = 946 mi (1,523 km); Mab = 6 mi (10 km)

NEPTUNE: Triton = 1,678 mi (2,700 km)

ACTIVE ENCELADUS

The bright surface of the small moon Enceladus is covered in snow that hides most of its impact craters. Saturn's powerful gravity turns the ice on Enceladus to liquid water just beneath the surface, and sometimes it bursts to the surface through cracks. This creates huge plumes of water vapor and snow that shoot up into space.

NOT TO MISS

MIMAS: *This moon looks like the "Death Star" from the* Star Wars™ *films thanks to its huge crater, named Herschel (see below).*

ENCELADUS: *The snow from its geysers gives this moon the brightest surface in the solar system.*

TETHYS AND DIONE: *Two mid-sized icy worlds with bright surfaces cracked by impact craters*

HYPERION: *This moon's sponge-like structure and chaotic spin suggest that it is all that remains of a much larger moon destroyed in an ancient collision.*

IAPETUS: *The dark patches on this strange satellite are thought to be material left behind when bright ice evaporated from its surface.*

PHOEBE: *This dark, icy satellite seems to be a giant comet that has been captured by Saturn's gravity.*

On Enceladus, blue tiger stripes mark warmer areas of water under the icy crust. Weak points on the surface allow the water to break through and boil away into space.

Titan

Saturn's satellite Titan is possibly the most complex moon in the solar system. It has a thick atmosphere, a landscape that resembles Earth, and even rain and snow! But it's also a deep-frozen world with an alien chemistry, and its similarities to Earth are skin-deep.

▌▌ METHANE MOON

Titan's dense orange atmosphere hides its surface from view. Most of the atmosphere is made up of nitrogen just like Earth's air, but the orange haze in its atmosphere comes from methane. Scientists think that this deep-frozen moon is at just the right temperature for methane and other similar chemicals to exist in three forms—solid, liquid, and vapor—just like water on Earth. Methane vapor rises from the surface and condenses like steam to form clouds in the atmosphere. Droplets of methane fall back down onto the landscape as rain and snow.

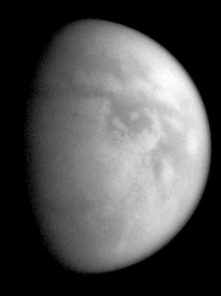

Titan orbits the planet Saturn once every 15 days and 22 hours.

▌▌ TRAVELER'S TIPS - TOURING TITAN

Titan is one of the strangest and most dangerous places in the solar system. Temperatures of -292°F (-180°C) aren't unusual, but the real danger comes from the ground and atmosphere. Parts of Titan are covered in frozen methane, creating enormous ice rinks. Other areas are slicks of slippery liquid methane, sticky tar, and other chemicals normally only found in oil reserves on Earth. You are likely to be soaked with a methane shower wherever you are. The atmosphere is highly flammable, and it's only the lack of oxygen that stops it from bursting into flames. You'll need to double check your oxygen tanks. One stray electrical spark and you're toast!

A MOON LIKE EARTH?

Once you've made it through Titan's hazy upper atmosphere, the landscape that opens up beneath you looks strangely similar to Earth's. Instead of the craters and sharp cliffs of Saturn's other moons, Titan has hills, valleys, rivers, and flat lake beds that sometimes fill with liquid methane. It's all the result of erosion— methane rain falling onto the ground wears away and smoothes out the land, just like water does on Earth. Some scientists think that Titan's similarities go farther and that the moon might even have developed its own primitive life.

This picture of Titan's surface was taken by the **Cassini Huygens** space probe in 2005. Scientists believe the rocks scattered around are actually frozen lumps of water ice.

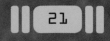

Uranus

Turquoise-colored Uranus is half the size of Saturn and twice as far from the Sun. Instead of light hydrogen gas, it's made up of heavier chemicals such as water, ammonia, and methane. Inside the planet, these chemicals form a slushy mix of ice and liquid, and for this reason Uranus is often called an "ice giant."

WORLD ON ONE SIDE

Perhaps the strangest thing about Uranus is its tilt. It was probably hit by another large object early in its history, and now it spins around the Sun while tipped over on one side. From the right angle, it's like looking at a target, with the fairly featureless planet as the bull's eye, framed by its family of thin rings. As Uranus orbits the Sun every 84 years, different parts of the planet are exposed to the light or plunged into darkness for long periods, giving it a unique pattern of seasons.

Uranus's ring system consists of narrow, dark rings mostly made of frozen methane. Astronomers discovered the system when the rings passed in front of a star, causing the star's light to flicker.

Uranus has at least 27 moons, but most are just captured asteroids or comets—only five are big enough to be worth a visit. In order from the planet outward, these are Miranda, Ariel, Umbriel, Titania, and Oberon. Each is made from a mix of ice and rock. Titania and Ariel both have bright patches, suggesting they may once have had frozen volcanoes that ooze slushy ice onto the surface. Miranda is amazing—a jumbled mishmash of a moon that was almost torn apart by Uranus's gravity at some point in the past.

NOT TO MISS

THIN RINGS: *Uranus is surrounded by about 13 rings. Much narrower than Saturn's rings, the widest ring measures just a couple miles across.*
TITANIA: *The largest of Uranus's moons, Titania (see below) has a spectacular system of deep canyons that make it well worth a visit!*
MAB: *One of Uranus's smaller satellites, Mab was discovered by the Hubble Space Telescope in 2003.*
FEELING COLD: *If you love the cold, Uranus is the planet for you. Temperatures of 88 degrees above absolute zero, which is about -371°F (–224°C), make it the coldest planet in the solar system.*

Scientists believe that Miranda melted under intense heat created by the effects of Uranus's gravity. This rearranged the moon's surface into a chaotic pattern.

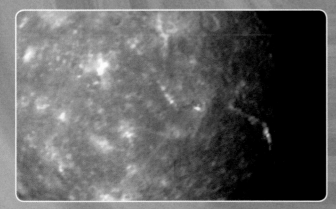

Neptune

Lurking in the gloom of the outer solar system, deep-blue Neptune looks like it is covered by a vast ocean of water. However, like Uranus, this world is an ice giant. Three thin rings surround Neptune and it has a family of moons —plus Triton, a big, captured visitor!

STRANGE SATELLITE

Neptune has a few small moons close in and a few orbiting comets much farther out. In between these is big, icy, and active Triton. It probably started out as a small world in its own orbit around the Sun before a close encounter saw it captured by Neptune's gravity. As Triton barged its way in, the original middle moons were scattered in all directions and are now lost forever.

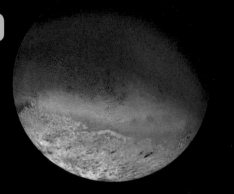

Triton's surface is made up of a crust of frozen nitrogen over an icy mantle, believed to cover a core of rock and metal.

TRAVELER'S TIPS - SIGHTSEEING ON TRITON

Triton probably started out as a dwarf planet like Pluto (see pages 28–29), but its encounter with Neptune really messed things up. As Triton was forced into its new orbit, Neptune's gravity pulled it this way and that, heating up and melting its icy surface. Ice volcanoes erupted and recovered much of the surface while rising blobs of warmer ice in some areas created lumpy terrain. Triton has not yet calmed down completely. Gas escapes from underneath the ice through geysers, forming weak jets several miles high. These jets are caught up in the strong crosswinds and blown around the planet. Sooty falling dust will blow straight into your visor, so clean off your space suit after your visit!

WORLD OF STORMS

Neptune gets very little heat from the Sun, but chemical changes deep inside the planet create a lot of energy. This helps power violent weather. Dark storms, or "dark spots," form in the lower atmosphere while bright, fast-moving clouds called "scooters" zip around above them, moving at speeds up to 1,305 miles per hour (2,100 km/h). Neptune has the fastest winds in the entire solar system, so keep a tight hold of your belongings! The planet's color comes from methane in its atmosphere. This soaks up red light from the Sun so Neptune only reflects blue light.

This huge dark spot in Neptune's atmosphere is a raging hurricane roughly 8,100 miles (13,000 km) across—about the diameter of Earth. The scooter clouds above it are thought to be made up of methane ice.

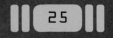

Comets

Comets are the loners of the solar system—rare visitors that spend most of their time lurking beyond Neptune's orbit. Occasionally they plunge toward the Sun and the inner planets in a headlong rush that sees them blaze into life for a few brief months.

RETURN VISITORS

Comets visiting the inner solar system usually follow long orbits lasting thousands of years that keep them far from the Sun most of the time. But if they come close to one of the giant planets, their orbits can be changed and they revisit the Sun more frequently. Halley's Comet, the most famous comet of all, returns every 76 years. It is next due around the Sun in 2061, but you may be able to see it on the outer edge of its orbit just beyond Neptune.

A comet has a bright nucleus with one or more tails streaming into space behind it.

TRAVELER'S TIPS - TAKE COVER!

Comets hurtle past the planets at enormous speed, and collisions are bound to happen sooner or later. In 1908, a comet exploded above the remote forests of Tunguska, Siberia, flattening 80 million trees across an area of 772 square miles (2,000 sq km). In 1994, Comet Shoemaker-Levy 9 plunged into Jupiter, creating the biggest explosion ever seen in the solar system. And 65 million years ago, it was probably a comet slamming into the present-day Gulf of Mexico that finished off the dinosaurs. Comet impacts are dangerous, unpredictable, and inevitable, so scientists are working on ways to destroy comets from a distance or divert them harmlessly around Earth.

The nucleus of a comet, often called a "dirty snowball," is made up of rock, dust, and water ice. Jets of vapor begin to erupt from the nucleus as it heats up on the approach to the Sun.

INSIDE A COMET

The solid heart, or nucleus, of a comet is usually a ball of dirty ice a couple miles across with a coating of dark soot. As it approaches the Sun and heats up, the ice starts to melt and evaporate, bursting through the surface in jets and forming a huge cloud of gas around the nucleus, called the coma. As dust and ice from the comet meet the solar wind of particles streaming out from the Sun, they are blown backward to form one or more tails that always point away from the Sun itself.

Beyond the Planets

The frozen depths of the solar system beyond Neptune are far from empty. They are filled with countless icy bodies ranging from dwarf planets just a little smaller than the real thing down to comets in long, slow orbits that never stray toward the Sun.

INTO THE KUIPER BELT

From just beyond Neptune's orbit, the solar system is surrounded by a ring-shaped region called the Kuiper Belt. A lot of comets reach the outer limits of their orbits here, but it's also home to much larger "Kuiper Belt Objects"—the icy equivalent of the asteroids. Some of these are officially classed as "dwarf planets." These include Pluto, which used to be considered the ninth planet but has now been downgraded to a dwarf planet. They take centuries or even thousands of years to orbit the Sun. Despite their small size, they often have quite large moons.

Pluto is made of rock and ice and is two-thirds of the diameter of Earth's Moon. It has three satellites of its own— Charon (above left), Nix (above right), and Hydra (not shown).

The planetoid Sedna is the coldest, most distant known object in the solar system. It stays at least three times farther away from the Sun than Pluto. It also has its own moon.

NOT TO MISS

HAUMEA: *A dwarf planet about one-third the size of Pluto, Haumea is shaped like a football.*
MAKEMAKE: *Another dwarf planet located in the Kuiper Belt at the edge of the solar system; Makemake was only discovered in 2005 (see below).*
CHARON, NIX, AND HYDRA: *Pluto's system of three moons*

EDGE OF THE SOLAR SYSTEM

It's hard to pinpoint exactly where the solar system ends. The effect of particles streaming out from the Sun comes to an end somewhere in the Kuiper Belt, but its gravity is still felt over much greater distances. There probably aren't any other planet-sized objects orbiting out there in the darkness, but there is a huge cloud of a trillion or more comets. This is the Oort Cloud, and it lies between 200 and 2,000 times farther out than Neptune. It is at the very limit of the Sun's gravity, already a quarter of the way to the nearest star.

Glossary

Astronomical body
A physical object in outer space, such as a comet, moon, planet, star, or asteroid (a space rock)

Atmosphere
The thin band of gases around a planet or a moon

Comet
An astronomical body that travels around the Sun; It consists of a solid, frozen nucleus that vaporizes on the approach to the Sun to form a glowing coma and tails of gas and dust.

Geyser
A jet of hot liquid or gas that shoots up under pressure through a crack in the crust of a planet or moon

Gravity
The force of attraction that astronomical bodies exert on each other as a result of their mass; The more massive they are, the stronger the gravitational force.

Moon
A natural body that orbits around a planet; For example, Earth has one moon while Mars has two.

Orbit
The curved path of an object around another, such as a planet around a star

Planet
An object that follows its own orbit around a star and is massive enough to be rounded into a spherical shape by its own gravity

Plate
One of several huge slabs of rock that make up the crust of a planet or moon; Known as tectonic plates, these slabs float on molten rock and interact with neighboring plates at their boundaries.

Satellite
A physical object in space, such as a moon, orbiting around a planet or star; Man-made satellites include devices placed in orbit around Earth to relay scientific or communications data.

Solar system
The Sun together with the eight planets —Mercury, Venus, Earth, Mars, Jupiter, Saturn, Uranus, and Neptune—and the other astronomical bodies that orbit it

Volcano
An opening in a planet or moon's crust which allows lava (molten rock), ash, and gas to escape from below the surface

World
A term for an astronomical body, typically a planet or moon; Our world, Earth, is a small, rocky planet.

Resources

BOOKS

Gas Giants: Huge Far Off Worlds
by David Jefferis
(Crabtree Publishing, 2009)

Graphing the Universe
by Deborah Underwood
(Heinemann Library, 2009)

The Far Planets
by Ian Graham
(Smart Apple Media, 2008)

The Universe: The Outer Planets
by Tim Goss and Geza Gyuk
(Heinemann Library, 2008)

QUICK QUIZ

Here are three quick-fire questions to test
your knowledge of the outer planets.
(Answers at the bottom) Good luck!

1. Which is the biggest moon? Is it:
 a) Earth's Moon
 b) Ganymede
 c) Titan

2. What lies beneath Europa's crust? Is it:
a) frozen sulfur
b) oil
c) liquid water

3. How many Earths would fit into
Jupiter's Red Spot? Is it:
a) 3
b) 10
c) 25

WEB SITES

www.planetary.org/home
A web site packed with information about the
planets, the exploration of the solar system,
and the search for extraterrestrial intelligence

www.universetoday.com
Space exploration and astronomy news
brought to you from around the Internet

www.nasa.gov/audience/forstudents
Scientists from NASA (National Aeronautics
and Space Administration) answer your
questions on the universe.

www.space.com
Information on everything to do with space—
satellites, stars, astronomy, the Sun, planets,
NASA, and more

www.spaceplace.nasa.gov/en/kids/
Out-of-this-world space puzzles, quizzes, and
activities to test your knowledge of the
solar system's planets and moons

www.kidsastronomy.com
A comprehensive guide to the universe with
interactive features and games

Quiz Answers: 1. b 2. c 3. a

Index